For Sam   V.T.
For Mum and Dad   M.M.

Text by Victoria Tebbs
Illustrations copyright © 2006 Melanie Mitchell
This edition copyright © 2006 Lion Hudson

The moral rights of the author and illustrator
have been asserted

A Lion Children's Book
an imprint of
Lion Hudson plc
Wilkinson House, Jordan Hill Road,
Oxford OX2 8DR, England
www.lionhudson.com
UK ISBN: 978 0 7459 4900 0
US ISBN: 978 0 8254 7884 0

First edition 2006
This printing September 2009
10 9 8 7 6 5 4 3 2 1

A catalogue record for this book is available
from the British Library

Typeset in 36/40 Baskerville MT Schoolbook

Printed and bound in Singapore
by Tien Wah Press (Pte) Ltd

Distributed by:
UK: Marston Book Services Ltd, PO Box 269,
Abingdon, Oxon OX14 4YN
USA: Trafalgar Square Publishing, 814 N Franklin
Street, Chicago, IL 60610
USA Christian Market: Kregel Publications, PO Box
2607, Grand Rapids, MI 49501

See and Say!
Christmas Story

Victoria Tebbs

Illustrated by Melanie Mitchell

LION
CHILDREN'S

Mary and Joseph go to Bethlehem.

clip clop clip clop

tweet-tweet

Poor Mary. She's so tired.
But there's no room to stay.

meow

'Yes, there is. You can come in here,' says the innkeeper.

Soon, Baby Jesus is born.

Awah! Awah!

Look – angels are in the sky.

baaa

la-la-la!

'Go to Bethlehem to see
the baby!' they say.

The shepherds go to see.

baa

Wise men bring presents.
'These are for the baby.'

Everyone loves Baby Jesus –
God's special baby.